Sophia Alexandra – **Summer on the Subway**

Sophia Alexandra

SUMMER ON THE SUBWAY

Poetry

PalmArtPress

Berlin

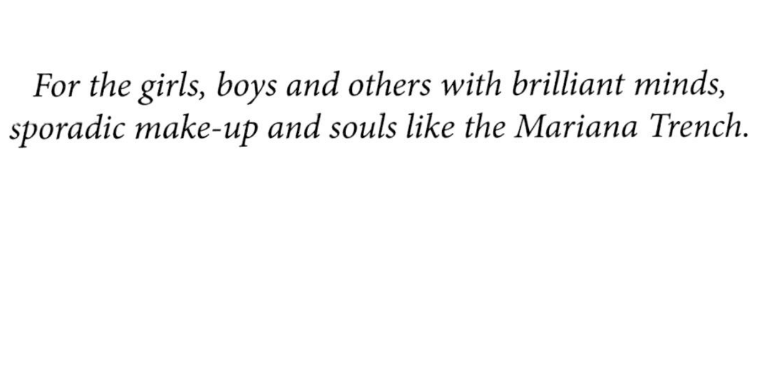

*For the girls, boys and others with brilliant minds,
sporadic make-up and souls like the Mariana Trench.*

*Maybe the sun keeps coming up because it has gotten used to you
and your constant need for proof.*

– Bright Eyes

2012

Poetry

drowning in the mist of sorrow
and soothing it with
the burning of smoke
in my lungs

it may sound like poetry
but it is none

poetry
is the voice in your head
that tells your heart
yes we can, we can move on
and rejoice happiness
every time
anytime

poetry
is the sound of church bells
in midnight air
when you're lying in bed
drifting

poetry
is the cup of tea at 8 in the morning
when you finally
got your shit together
and woke up early

poetry
is the laundry and cooking at noon
and dancing and singing
to that song you secretly like
and all your friends despise

poetry
is working and making
and simply creating
and smiling and running
and "god, you look stunning"
when you finally got off
your diet of wine and cigarettes

poetry
is you and me and our sweat
and tears and laughter
our fears and our strength
to bend them and brake them
and give them away

poetry
is in the color you mix
for your hair
and the water that rinses it off

and poetry
is in the hands that comb it
not too often, but now they do
tired hands, gentle hands
mother's hands

love
is
in poetry

And I'm Shivering Cold On A Well-Lit Stage

there's been silence for a while now

but not in my head
no
at night those words rage
against my eyelids
they flourish and grow into
a carnivorous plant
eat me up
swallow me whole

when your body unites against you
it should be crystal clear that
you either have to change
your venomous, excruciating, catastrophic
ways
or
just go to hell straight away

I am still deciding

I probably will be forever
today I'm indifferent
yesterday I was sure of my victory
over myself, over you
over the world

I'm pretty sure tomorrow
I'll either discover immunity
(happiness)
or just recite the lines

of this empty book
I've been writing
over and over
and
over
again
I wonder why I even keep
moving the pen
(a blank page)
tear the blank page of the novel
you've been reading
out

that first, or last one
fascinated me most
all my life
and I never had the courage
to fill it
with the beauty of silver lined love

(that   will   change)

Konzert

no service, the point at which you are
lost
cut off from reality
a foggy sky mending into
the raging bloody ocean
the lone guitar laying in machine gun
pose
the audience forgets its importance

I have sailed too long and stopped
too often
placed the anchor in seaweed and sand
met with the risk of sliding away
so many times

I'm not sure why or when I will arrive
or if there is a place to that arrival
all I know is I am restless
reckless
mindless
daring to say I have no regrets

light me up, I am not human
even the stray dogs can sniff it
they stare at me, in disbelief, who is she
who, or what
when I walk away the empty space
that held my body
keeps them looking into nothingness
who or what or where or when
not why

Potential

why won't you keep your apartment clean and your fridge stocked
We are worried.
why don't you just get up and do the dishes and why don't you
ride a bike or stretch or do something for your health exercise
is so good for your body and it will make you happy too and
you have always been lazy but you are so smart and you can
overcome anything so why aren't you when you were a child you
would start things but never finish them you would lose interest so
quickly maybe we should have pushed you to focus on something but
you were always so adamant in what you wanted and I thought you
knew what was best for you why don't you know how to write an
annotation of a book why don't you just do it when you are so smart
as a child your teachers said you would be so much more you had
such potential why don't you use your potential you are in the top
ten percent of people in IQ but you can't eat before you get dizzy
We are worried.
why do you fall apart without your partner why are you so childish
why can't you work and study and clean and eat and dream and love
and see the world go to shit and witness the apathy of seventy percent
of the people you meet and be kind and be intelligent and be rational
and be fit and not be so perfectionist it really stands in your way and
go out more and take care of yourself and care less about others but
have a decent amount of friends and be happy and just be happy and
make breakfast and deal with the mortality of all your loved ones in
the span of five years and do laundry and go to the streets for basic
civil rights for people in different countries or with different skin
because so many people are fucked in the head and somehow don't
believe in that and also divide your trash because we are polluting
the earth and humans are monsters anyways but goddamnit be happy
why can't you just be a bit more like we would like ourselves to be
We are worried.

This Is Me

this is me pouring words into empty spaces
this is me shivering in coldest summer rain

this is me and i love and i breathe and i smile
this is me and i cry and i walk in circles all the time
this is me and i am reckless and mindless and fearless
this is me and i am running through fields and being

naive
this is me

and i am a liar a sinner a thief
i am a beauty and hideous and mean this is me

and i have this huge heart that beats
and my tambourine feet that leap

this is me falling into repetitive patterns again and
braking with what i had to fight and
this is me redefining wrong and right and
embracing former evil
this is me changing
this is me aging

me

  shape shift thing

this is me and i don't feel any different

this is me
        and let me be it

Timeless

tick tock
the clock
rewinds
in my head

back to that moment when
we threw our hats
and our colors went flying
such joy, such joy
I don't recall throughout
the years
back to that moment when
all I did was smile
and congratulate
and be congratulated
it stops at the point where
I found you standing
in the crowd
and we hesitated
before that embrace

tick tock
the clock
rewinds
in my head

back to that moment I saw
your face over mine
your eyes locked
in my gaze
your naked arms
the lines of your body

tick tock
the clock
rewinds
in my head

back to your hand
clinging on to mine
your smell on that rooftop
the warmth of your body
comforting me

tick tock
the clock
rewinds
in my head

back to us laughing
on our way to fresh pond

tick tock
the clock
moves on

You

blue I guess is not enough
to be a mermaid
your hair needs to be long
and wavy like the ocean
but no worries darling
we're getting there
and then my kiss can save you
from all the tears you're
drowning in
a sea of salt and beauty
take my hand
and swim
through the mighty
depths of truth
learn to breathe without air
and walk on groundless eternity
fly love, it's easy, really
fly with that sparkling fire of yours
water and flames are friends
in a mermaids kingdom
we dance with the sounds
of happy madness
join us
join us
the song of the sirens

Nails On Parchment

no words, no more my love
I lost them all in the process of losing
you
and now I'm trying to
redefine them in complete darkness

I just hope this is paper
I am writing on
and not my flesh
but then again what difference
would it make
just adding trashy letters
to the scars on my chest

I am tired and empty and
need I desperately need
to rest
but I'm sleepless without you
holding my thoughts
and carefully untangling them
you were so good at keeping me sane

it's over love, it's over
the pain is over now
rushed into muscles and bones
instead of breaking a heart

your eyes wrote poetry
in my soul
your words painted my
starry starry van Gogh night

I miss the warmth of your arms
around me
and the security of that embrace
I miss your lips resting on mine
your eyes a question mark
they already held the answer
I saw it, did you?

„I love you", you said
and I finally allow myself
to cry
one tear an achievement
of importance
for now

Cannonball

nothing compares
to the joy you feel
when your past is lifted
into the electrified air
black and gray, bouncing
like visualized dubstep
for a moment
a golden 12 flickers
through the seconds of satisfied
accomplishment
and you're part of a laughing
cheering, glowing mass of
beauty
arms shooting up towards the sky
and coming back down
to embrace earth
you can feel the dreams
in the air, the lightning
strikes between the bodies
cloaked in coal
someone threw a match
and finally
lit us up

She Had A Shadow

for Shiala after Joy Harjo

She had a shadow.

She had a shadow that was made out of smoke.
She had a shadow that was soaked in chloroform.
She had a shadow that was made out of storm.
She had a shadow that was crawling out of the ocean
and back in again.

She had a shadow.

She had a shadow that rained in color.
She had a shadow that had blue skin.
She had a shadow that was a blonde
and tall tattooed woman.
She had a shadow that cast out the day.

She had a shadow.

She had a shadow that grew wings to outfly her.
She had a shadow that was spun from laced fabric.
She had a shadow that ran from her
and one that held her tight.

She had a shadow.

She had a shadow that grew in sunlit gardens.
She had a shadow that fought eternal wars.
She had a shadow that prayed for the devil.
She had a shadow that got lost in the moonlight.

She had a shadow.

She had a shadow made out of waves of music.
She had a shadow dripping of loneliness.
She had a shadow full of butterflies
that would haunt her in the darkness.

She had a shadow for each life.

2013

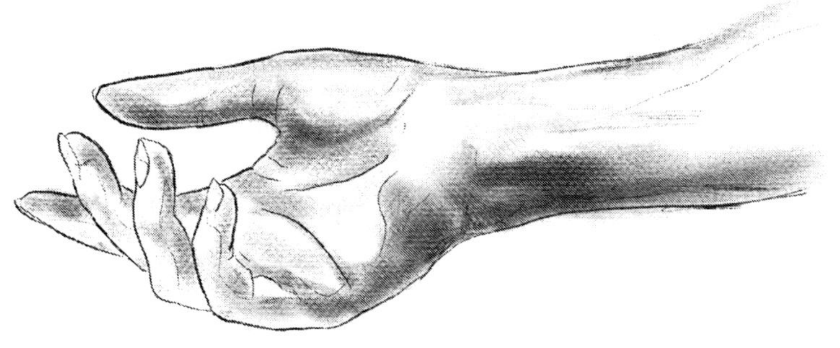

Lantern Heart

The sky is a dark dark indigo
and your smell lingers in the breeze of May

I love you

and you didn't run, and you didn't turn away.

Bells and Sand

there's something about
the ringing of church bells
when I am high up in this Rapunzel room
even before *High Hopes* I just felt
magical
when they reminded me of the ancient
hands and bodies that made them

there's something about
churches in their state of being
those sacred buildings
that have taught me to wonder
and that there are things
more powerful than me
even though I do not
subscribe to the concept
their power is used for

I believe in the myth of the brick walls
and the magic of the sand that
was compressed into them
and the water that floats in their
bases

a conjunction
of life
in a building
and silence
and awe

Soul Marches

the barren land
between here and the ocean
between fire and liquid
between you and my soul
the barren land
between the burning fields
that are your werewolf eyes
inked darkness
fading into colors
of your heart
the land between
the traces of smoke
around your smile
and my mermaid eyes
we call it the soul marches
cause you wander around
lost
forever attempting to reach
the other side

Two O One One

two o one one
life passes in fragments
and I
sway into nostalgia at London Eye
where sounds mend into the Thames
and my heart mends into the sky

memories vibrating through guitar strings
fingertips and eyeballs
pulsating pupils, staring
oh bring me
bring me back to life

two o one one
marble lions spread their wings over Venice
and I
fall asleep in Charles-H.-King Street
with the stars in my eyes

two o one one
the alternative pigeons fly high over Luther Square
and I
fall into a pit of ever present beauty
where happiness and love shine brighter

two o one one
the street artists blur into the setting sun
and I
let go, let go, let each of you go
I loved you, I loved you, I loved you so

I Cry Babel, Babel Look At Me Now

Silver lined fabric
The promise of a home, somebody to love
A question posed into thin air

Breathing

Crystallized touch, movements of a dancer
The fallacious dress floating

You are the night
You are the ocean

Cloaked with nightingale feathers
Clinging onto the hands of
A brave man with a lonesome heart

People are like stardust you say
Shimmering, gone too soon and
impossible to forget
I wish everyone thought like you sometimes

Silence

While the fog keeps crawling
A wolf's howl in the distance
Radiant faces dipped in sunlight

Laughter

None of this needs to stop

2014

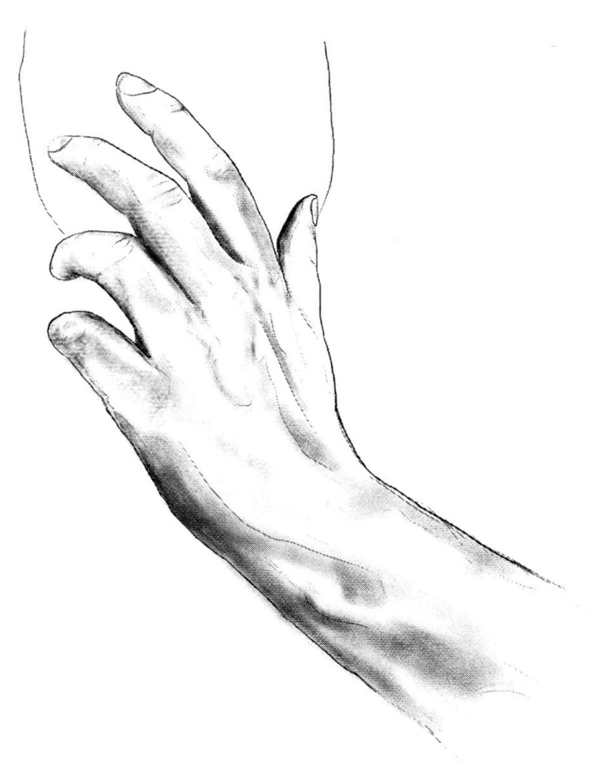

1

a painter
I would have to be a painter
for now that I am not heartbroken
my poetry seems to draw blurry pictures
unlike the clarity I used to love
it is so hard to live in this stage of beginning again and not having ended yet
I feel like a something
not unhappy
nor overly happy
and not at all empty
and not at all full
it's like I am this *thing* that has no definition
forcing my poetry to have none as well
no end just beginnings I am full of beginnings and I believe endings are overrated as such
life is an accumulation of moments
and none of them end
they just blur into another
like explosions of color
like pieces of string

2

where is my mind is quite the question
if you believe in solving such a riddle, it's preposterous
a child in a haze, a mouse in a maze, pebbles in a waterfall
what is my mind
thorns in an avalanche, painting with *all the colors of the wind*, grey corridors
my psychiatrist Harleen has packed her bags, she
is off to see the world
and loose the madness
hypothetical statistics drive me crazy
I lose my sleep at night
have been so many people things and places
where is my mind

2015

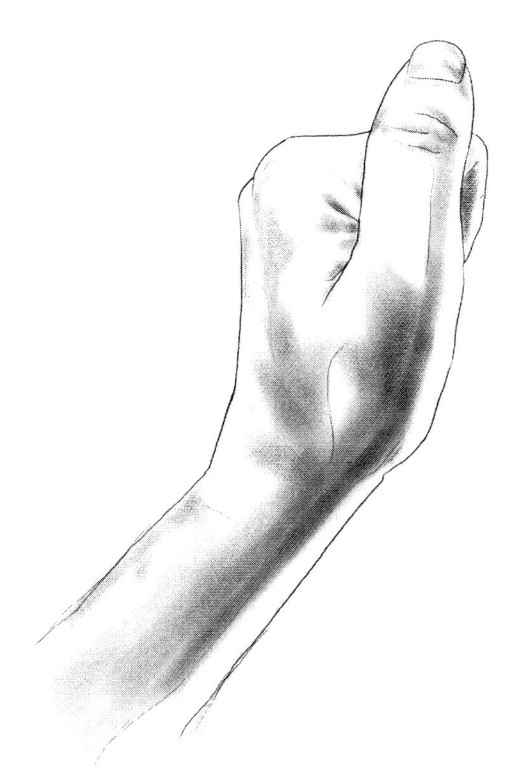

Out In The Open

a battle fought in shattered armor
right hand cut off –
learned to fight with the left
you were the first sword of Braavos
in another life
now you're banned into the shadows
of your own demon heart

trembling with all your insides
but keeping it together on your skin
just your eyes – this
doorway to your soul, what a cliché
thing to say – just your eyes they
pace back and forth and still you
put all of your everything into
making them shine
with determination
and happiness
and never
giving
up
!
and you hold on to
tumbling rocks in an avalanche
while you fall and you
stutter and stumble
but
come to a rest
in a paradise of destruction
where you set your bones
pick up a pebble
and start rebuilding your castle
on newly born
ground

I Loved You, Goodbye

Carry on my wayward son
There'll be peace when you are done ...
Don't you cry no more

– Kansas

lay your weary head to rest now

my moon and stars my sunshine

I have taken a turn too many

into the realms of my wounded jealous egoistic heart

sometimes we are blind to see

what beauty lies in the ever-present now

smiles taken for granted

forgive me

forgive me

now

I sleep like a baby in other people's beds

and their breaths whisper their stories in dark grey and faded blue pastel

yours was caged light and sunshine maybe

my cotton wool antennas could sense the broken frequencies of your reality

I was hoping to descend into your dreams and save you

the naiveté of every girl I guess

frustrated from never succeeding I am

giving you up now

and hoping your insides wont

crumble like mine did

hoping I didn't hold you together

like you held me

forgive me if I did

forgive me

now

A

when the rhythm of a song is beating
knife-cuts
hearts flesh
I bleed memories
through sedatives

it's what we are it's all
we are
reality is a concept
I have yet to understand
but I am closer to it
than I have ever been

I thought I'd be a child
forever
and now I'm standing here
almost a woman

B

white clouds again
and after all of this fear
I feel the thrill of the rush
of the happy freedom
at take-off
myself again blazed in crystal sunlight
the atmosphere is toxic
here
that is thinner
that is empty
my heart skips into
loopholes of air, I
transform, transcend
expand into the missing
spots of oxygen
my mind is vibrant
that is lonely
in the best way
solitude is welcome
after
what feels like years
of love and laughter
a couple days
my darling
so I can rejoice the sweet
flow of pouring
dripping sunlight
in your smile when I
see you again

C

I am
supermassive atoms rotating in angular circles trough luminescent alleys
of matter sprinkled over the universe like snow at sundown when the
light turns colors yet to be named
I am
singular pieces of a puzzle dazzled in glitter, dust and earthquakes
I am
angels wings made of raindrops in crystalline sugar
I am
you I am you I am you

Self

I am who
And what
I am
With bags under my eyes
Tired
Scared
Exhilarated
Jaws clenched
In love with the world
I will not apologize
I will not paint
Over life
Reflecting on my skin
I will not be perfect
I refuse

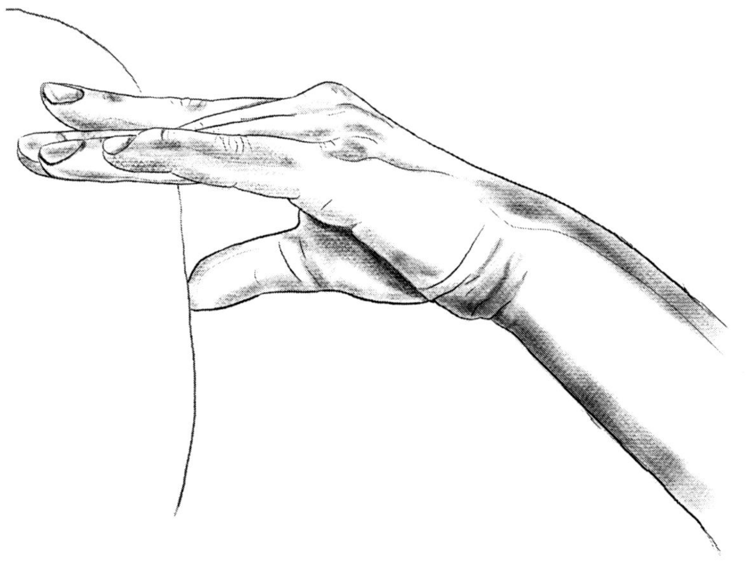

Spring Came

for Rudi

spring came in the wake of your death
and I didn't cry as much as I could have
should have
something about the sun turns everything golden
I never knew what it felt like for someone to just
not be there ever again
it is a concept so foreign I wonder
how it could be imprinted in my nature
maybe humans have evolved too much
the brain capable of understanding
incapable of processing
I don't know if science could support my claim
you would have
I always thought I would be upset with the world
would find it unfair that a genius can go while a
million braindead others can stay
I don't
it feels blissfully irrelevant
how life isn't fair because it doesn't have to be
balance is a manmade concept
my cat doesn't care that
the moth still had reason to live
the flowers grow lilac and pink
yellow and auburn
they rise and thrive
to the sound of
the piano

This City

this city is a nightmare factory
clenched in a haze of filthy dreams
sunrise sundown
wake up turn around
repeat

I rush from project to project
keeping myself occupied in jumbles of work
sometimes paid mostly unpaid but
essential for existing

they deflect from the ever
present need to run
from the cities gaping holes of solitude
bodies piled atop each other
held together by
hopes dangling from silk threads
twisted minds concealing daggers
swords and guillotines by
piling them up in plain sight
the streets are cluttered with them
paved with spilled blood and sweat

Psychological Analysis Of Life

Loneliness is a toxin
Depression is a side effect of anxiety
Pills can only numb but never take away pain
If there is no pain to take away
You can't use pills to cure the void

July

too much has happened
to go forward
and the way back has collapsed
left solid concrete wreckage
spilled all over
any path or road
I have been standing on this platform between
nothing and my ruins
the wind slowly etching into me
the rain slowly forming canyons on my skin
the sun dries them up
the rain falls again
my heart desperately beats and beats
with an unclenching will to live
to leap forward
if only there was land in sight
if only there was something
anything
to leap to
I am a molecule floating in a vacuum
ten thousand times my size
no way of controlled movement in any direction
no way of standing still
no idea which gravity is keeping me afloat
faint dreams of pebbles falling and distant
waterfalls
I wonder if this inner rebellion
is a presage of them fading
into null

Tablanet

за дядо

when you left it was raining
and my mother wailed and screamed but all her
anger couldn't help her
you would not have cared for the fuss made
over a corpse
you would not have cared if I said goodbye
you would have taken my hand in yours
and told me about Vehlow
and how the women thought you were my father
driving me around
in our red Honda
I don't know if you liked cats
I don't know much really
just that we would play cards and chess
and you would always win
until I started winning and then I knew
it wasn't because of my growing skill
but because of your mind
slowly betraying you
I used to be sad about it
I wasn't anymore
not for years now
you kissing my hand
was enough
to know that you loved me
love me still
you'll never be gone
to me

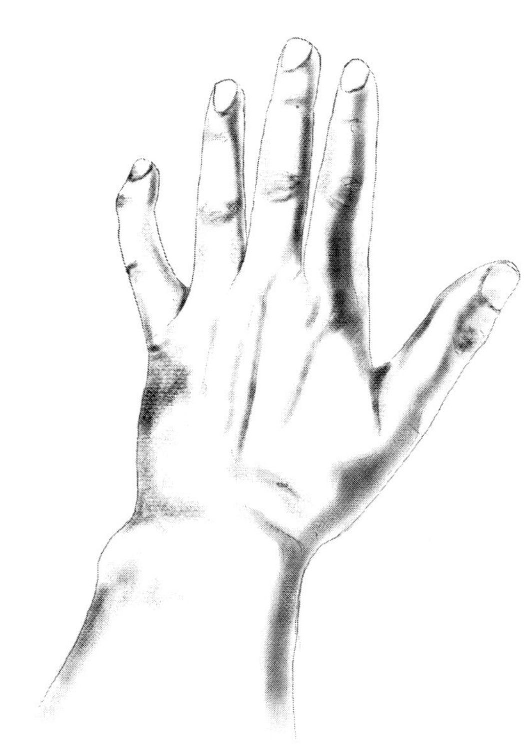

April

I am remarkably clairvoyant
but forget all the prophecies in an instant
I am the people to my own Cassandra
in constant dialogue
asking myself why did this happen
when it was so clear that it would

poetry is a like a mason jar
conserving feelings that can still
touch you
after what feels like a million years

and what doesn't feel like a million years really
time spins infinity that blurs into one
in this moment I am twenty-two summers
I am a second
momentarily combining the history of the universe
in the matter of my skin
the electrical signals in my brain carry the roaring echo
of the big bang

it is necessary to fall apart so you can be found
sometimes
especially if you are so set on getting it right

I have trained for perfection all my life
I am only just learning
to be flawed
to listen to prophecies
to not be ashamed of
staying naive

Metaphors

I don't want
to lose myself
to this
so, I end up
screaming at the
top of my lungs
hoping
the distant echo will be heard
hoping I will be saved
when all I have to do is
save myself
and I have all the metaphors for it
just jump
jump off your platform and see
how you fall
the trouble is
metaphors are not
what life is made of
and I don't know
how
to jump

August

tiny creatures of wonder
in a stargazing moment preserved
in time
raspberry fields
chiming laughter
echoing through eternity
light years from now

distance equals time
equals life

time equals life
equals love

your hand is the gentility
I have received from everyone else

is with me now
in this multiverse
untangled
for my third birthday

for my baby girl chasing butterflies
for me
it all blurs
it all pushes forward
around me
around
the sun

Laura

I might still call you Laura
maybe Lora
maybe Láura
maybe Aura even
Audra
Audry
my love
my darling girl
I will cherish you
I will let no harm come to you
we will inhale the ocean
every morning
I will build you a house made of
glass and timber
I will grow a rose garden
and let you see me
smile and linger
plant tranquility and kindness in your soul
I will not have ambition
other than the ambition to
keep away pressure
I will love you
I will love you always
and I will be so
that you can love me
too

Manifesto

the color of the ocean soothes me every time
accumulating the strength of a thousand yoga mantras
it is the only thing that will bring me
to a level of peace that lets me rest

I haven't felt as good in days

letting go of the flickering lights
of the hectic city skyline dancing in my veins
like Andersen's mermaid I
transform into dust and love and darkness
but reunite with who I am

I want life to be like a bungee jump
first we hesitate, we're scared and then
when the tickling curiosity overcomes our fear
we jump into troubles and choices, adventures and laughter
and adrenaline pumps through our bodies as we fall

sometimes we will regret being pulled back by the rope
we will struggle to fly
on occasion we will lose control
but mostly we will have seen the world in all of its beauty

and end up where we started

with eyes glowing and heads held high

Little Beast

1

fear plays catch with me
and I run from her
like a deer from the hunter
so many misunderstood years
pause, look me in the eye
I will not run
any
more

2

I have come to bargain
you and I, a white flag
we break the bread
a flayed being
winces, flees
do not be afraid of me
be angry, rebel
I won't fight anymore
both sides of the battlefield
lie crumbled in ashes
I am here
shoot me
or take my hand

Willkommensklassen

the moon over Aleppo
is silver and gigantic
at night
on the roof of Ahmads
home
it is warm
and one can gaze at its beauty

Saleh looks for his house
on Google earth
to show to his classmates
the house that no longer exists
along with everything else
Saleh shrugs and looks for
other pictures

Momo is an Instagram model and soccer player
here in Berlin
everyday life catches up with us quickly

Tzveta says
when the war is over
you will rebuild your house
and I will visit you
he beams, says:
"Truly?"
and
"Yes, I will rebuild."

sometimes when I close my eyes
I can hear the bombs
(1945 – now)

– but we cannot take them all in –
of course
the bombed-on kids
the infants on the rubber dinghies
the healthy men

      ■
           ■
                  ■
      ■
                 ■
     ˋˊ   ˋˊ

into our concrete block apartments
our architect-designed villas in Wannsee

XXXXXX refugees
a number on the news
– but you know not all of them are real refugees -
boom
boom
goes the rifle
by Heckler & Koch
in the safe country of origin
Afghanistan
in my head I can hear
the woman scream
your hashtag metoo on facebook
couldn't help her
but hey, me too
and it is a trauma for life
I do understand we cannot all
carry the weight of the world at all times

but Saleh is real
and so are Ahmad
and Momo
and I
dream of Aleppo

Aleppo Is A City In Syria

Aleppo is a city in Syria
I build it as a miniature set
Next to the ruins of Pellinor

Aleppo is like the buildings in Inception
Collapsing into the ocean to Hans Zimmers droning

Aleppo is like Astapor
Daenerys circles it with her dragons
I envision them flying
The bombs, the grenades

I have never seen a weapon
That is, I have seen at least 10000 weapons
But I have never seen a weapon
You know what I mean

I believe Syria is warm, like Astapor
How warm exactly I couldn't say
Like Phoenix? Hotter? Phoenix is my limit of
Heat imagination

In Death Valley I was scared to die of thirst
With 8 gallons of water in the trunk
I don't know what thirst is

I do know what fear is and
It is hard for me to justify that
As I think Aleppo knows fear better

When I close my eyes, my breath becomes dust
And children who play in it
Becomes careful carelessness
Becomes a father who pulls his son out of the rubble
Becomes Aleppo

I know absolutely nothing about pain
About fear
About courage and struggle

My mind builds Aleppo
To understand

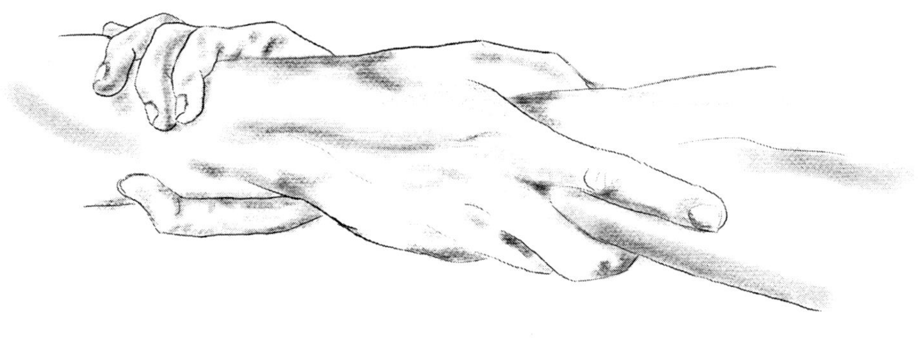

Greysky

you are
a grown woman now
as am I
and all these years of distance
stood between us
they flicker, they fade
into haze on snowy evenings in Albuquerque
and sunny nights in West Berlin
I love you still
I love you always
through cellophane colors
in liquid crystal oceans
over mountains of light

Strength

my father and I
held hands
on the bench
in front of
a pirate-ridden church
in the Spanish colonies
and we wept in silence
words were not needed
to describe what it is
to now
be the last father
to now
be the last child to a living father
to remember kindness, goodness, love
to hold each other
profusely, unendingly
hold on to each other
hold on to this
precious
life

Summer On The Subway

Coins spent on bread, alcohol, water or cigarettes
collected in an empty cardboard cup
I lend money from my future self
and my mother says
You can't give to everyone
you are not that rich
Aren't I?
Money spent on a son's smile for Christmas
to satisfy addiction
My grandmother says
Don't play with the Roma
they are filthy and dirty
you will catch fleas
Marian and I climb high into the metal pyramids
set on crumbled concrete on the streets of Sofia
playgrounds made before safety regulations
when children were people
not raw eggs to be held in cotton wool and
broken when they're old enough
When are you old enough to break?
Marian laughs like the world is in his pocket
half a year of windchimes and sunlight
winter comes
I never see him again
I go on living my stationary white people life
What I'd give to catch a glimpse of a passing smile
that I could never recognize now

2 Hours And 56 Minutes

2 hours and 56 minutes
I send you on a google maps trip
with pinpoints, descriptions
2 hours and 56 minutes
of nonstop walking
are needed
to circle my life

2 hours and 56 minutes
to walk from hallowed halls
where I learned about hope
to a classroom on Broadway
where I learned about courage
to little benches in the Yard
where I learned about love
and most of all about loving myself
to Pecan Pie that used to symbolize coming home
but now only remains a Beacon of hope for returning
to Weeks at dusk when the lights dance between the cities
into moonlit nights where I can never send anyone
into longing that hasn't seized in seven years
my god

the weight on my chest
in my throat
on my eyes
is the smoke of D'Jarums
is the rooftop at Porter
is the stones that I carry
from the bank of the Charles
brought to me by a traveler
when I couldn't bear it
anymore

Epigenesis

Time's Up when it has been for decades
I feel the rape of my foremothers
in the depth of my bones
genetically embroidered on my skin
I feel the cruelty of my forefathers to my
brothers and sisters of color
of anything that wasn't them
in the tips of my fingers, stuck down
my throat, clenched in my jaws when I sleep
I am a descendant
I am a woman
I live and I breathe through history
that is violence
hoping to one day leave a world to my daughters
a world that is worthy of the meaning
of a word that is love

Decade

it came like a flood
creeping
rolling
seeping
into homes
into parks
it made us shut doors
paint red crosses
wear half a face
forget about friends

it humbled us
taught us resilience
it killed with a vengeance
it fractured
it healed

what it is to be human
oblivious
hopeful
against all odds
to find the good
to keep persisting
like weeds in a field
like flowers through snow

Of Viruses And Men

I sympathize with
your will to live
but must you

rampage through
the living

procreate in numbers
that cannot be sustained

kill the weak
the poor
and creep
into the depths of life

must you build
and accumulate
with no purpose
but destruction

until all is dead
and all is rotten
and you lie in the dirt

and you go down
with yourself

Another Spring Day In B Minor

I wish I had been old enough
mature enough
smart enough
less naïve
less oblivious
I wish I would have
appreciated
loved
cherished
called
you more

I wish you hadn't been
my introduction to death

sometimes I am convinced
you would have liked my work
it would have brought you joy
but now I'll never know
I'll never know because
I never bothered
I regret
I don't regret much
I regret
I never
bothered

the heart and mind of a teenager
you helped me at every turn
you would not talk much
would hand me to Dolores
I would find that weird

wouldn't know what to say
I wish I had just talked
talked your ear off
sent you postcards

I know you talked hours with her
and I wish you were here to still
make her happy
she is so sad sometimes

I wish I had come to visit
on my own
to drink green tea
sleep on the pull-out couch
to listen to music
to sit in silence
I wish

Wait For It

sometimes I
lose myself in imaginary tragedy
stages music
screen

I have to remind myself
I have a career that fulfills me
a relationship
that is a friendship
that is a passion
people I call friends

sometimes I forget
how far I've come
that I am not that
I don't know why
I go to extremes girl
anymore

that I have learned to breathe and
trace my heartbeat home
that I am safe
that I am healthy
that I am happy

that the news seem bleak but
that's because all they show is
bleakness
that there is light
that there is sun
that there is honesty love humanity
that I am not bitter

that I will not become bitter
that it is a joy
an unending present
to live

A Moment

for the poems
I wrote and deleted
single lines first
stanzas then
rewrote
restructured
tore to bits
emptied
pressed backspace
until they were
merely carcasses
torn to the bone
and picked clean

some things we dare not write
some things are better left unsaid

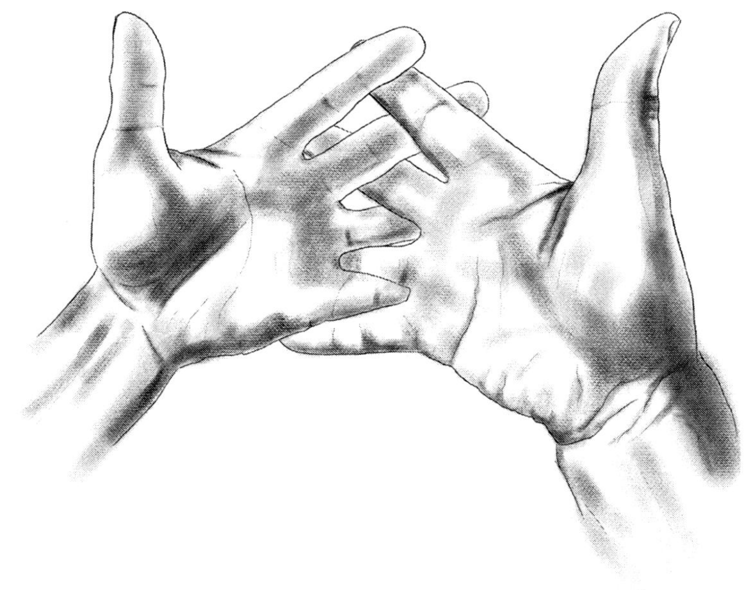

New Year's Eve

electrifying freedom came with curfew
and between champagne glasses and scattered fireworks
marvel and wonder returned to my soul

between Horo and Bulgarian TV pop songs
between hugs and kisses and joy
I found family is everything and love is all

Mowing The Lawn In May

Downeaster Alexa on guitar strings
It was so important to you that I got the rhythm right

Say goodbye to Hollywood in the back of a rental car
I was eleven, in love for the first time, amazed and
Lost in emotions of an intensity that I got from you
Even though you would say I got them from mom

It made you angry when I cried because of minor injuries
Minor mistakes, feelings, things that could be overcome
You showed me a clear path that I couldn't always follow
You carved it out and still it didn't always come as easy to me

But then you made my teddy bear talk well into my teens
And you still marvel at the squirrels jumping form tree to tree
Like a boy seeing them for the first time; you scold me
About my usage of plastic, my tiredness of caring

You hold me anyways, you held me always, no matter
You gave me arms to hold on to and a steady heartbeat to follow
And in airplanes and storms, in this world I am never lost
Never uneasy, when you have placed your hand on mine

And you act like people anger you, but you love so deeply
Hold out so loyally, would kill for my mother who would kill for you
That unwavering constant, that unending certainty has
Kept me steady during earthquake after earthquake all my life

Summer, Highland Falls in raspberry fields filled with laughter
And in non-talking car rides, hours upon hours of just singing
Of just being with you
I long to be with you every day now
Every day now

Adulthood

I always thought it was a fantasy
something I would never feel
or something that would happen
suddenly
jarringly
something cold and glaring
that would hurt the eyes
I would have to raise my hand
to shield from the phosphoric light
I thought I would be radically different
would lose myself in order to be earnest
and become rough around the edges
I wouldn't like myself anymore

it slipped into my world
like a warm blanket
like a comforting ray of sun
that untangled my thoughts
and gave my feelings meaning
and I became earnest and rough
gently and lovingly
I learned to take things seriously
when they deserved such respect
I learned that being soft and happy
meant having edges to protect that world
I nestled into it with a hot chocolate
and a blanket and felt at home in my life

I earned it through begging God or whatever entity
for the life of my mother kneeling on a church floor
through howling in the shower, muffled screams
whispers, *please save my father, I want nothing more*

through vowing to be worthy of such a gift
through vowing to be impactful, purposeful, kind
through self-forgiveness, through love
through accepting all people are people
and think and feel and breathe
through vowing to love life, to love air
to love love love
and knowing that love also means
knowing what you don't love
and never judging yourself for that
to become firmly secure in acceptance of self
even if you are insecure at times
to know that you will be insecure at times
to look back on your journey
and think
you were impulsive and shortsighted
like all children are
you were lovely and complicated
and you pushed forward and tried
you tried so very hard
for me

my cat yells at the shower
while I cry myself to peace
the small hours collide with
lingering hands entwined
each inch of skin
taken for granted in its'
exhilaratingly exorbitant familiarity

no matter the events my life
is a moderately paced art house drama
where I am extra number 5
and all my acquaintances in the peripheral
don't even have lines
up until your footsteps echo up the stairwell
and someone turns the camera on me

I need nothing new
have zero interest in adventuring onto new bodies
colliding in adrenalines of the uncertain
8 years, each day, each breath, each moment
airport sun downs, phone call train hours
up the nostrils face times
cascading into your heartbeat, your scent on the wind
I don't read anything new
I need you

War

we created a circus of worlds together last time we met
they played in Theatre Pushkin, actors, professors, mothers, fathers
little Anya laughs at the faces I make and stares at the musicians in awe
the acting students lay out their raw emotions in 45 minutes
fear
loss
monstrosity
humanity
new friends are made in the backyard of a summer party in Berlin
Sasha's hair has turned grey

Headfast

father has 2 hours between meals
his day is structured into time that is
constantly running away and
surviving

mother has 2 hours between cooking
her day is structured into time for
intellectual or exhausted thought and
loving

father smashes firewood with his pain
mother canalizes it into her jaw and feet

father and mother shower in sunlight
and bathe in the green of the garden
they relish in fulfilling work, don't see it as such
they stick together like glitter glue

evenings are islands of old normality
minutes and hours are borrowed from sleep

mother fights Goliath, tears at mile thick
gooey fabric, pulls at black tar to push free
father explodes against shattering glass
tries to not cut himself on the shards

there's so much fight in them I think
it is what has kept them alive
through all of this madness
there is so much love in them I think
it is what has kept me alive
through all of this madness

That Funny Feeling

full frontal impact with *That Funny Feeling*
somehow when it's Bo the hit home is muffled
the hand slapping you also extends to hold you
Phoebe – like a scalpel – precision strikes into
the mines under the dump of fallen skyscrapers remains
Gotham that I buried and paved over and
rinsed with soil and tried to drown out with flowers
some nights I just want to scream

T

for my husband

There is no need to write for you
Because you are in everything I write
Every metaphor has been said before
And we are in no need of metaphors
Just a steady inhale and exhale and time

June In The Foothills

sipping milk from a thick-walled glass
like a child with white-cornered lips
Tristan and Isolde prelude reaching its final momentum
I reread poems dissect them but
can't keep my mind in one place for too long
staring out at the medieval castle walls
in suburban southern Germany
this very undramatic garden turned
wildly romantic dramatically fantastic
Seashore by Moonlight
by a violin and a clarinet

my heart follows the strings in a way
that puts mere words on a page to shame
I burst into sound and seize to think
this is the closest we will ever come to magic

I am interrupted by an ad about pregnancy vitamins
it's all I keep getting lately, I married a man so I must
now be pregnant or at least want to be pregnant
or at least think about being pregnant
or if not then they have made it their mission to
press me into a societal cookie cutter shaped like a mom
will I ever be ready, ever feel ready, ever have done enough
ever think the time is right to be a mom

I am driven to work by an endless desire
to make something that will outlast me
to find fulfillment in art that seems enough
so the end of a project only leaves me thirstier
and there is an exhilaration in the thirst
that leads to an ignorance of the body

and by extension the mind in all its factettes
and so much goes into it that the pull on
the physical form becomes unpredictable

star crossed lovers dying from broken hearts
is what history frequently remembers
through dopamine hazed needs for laurels
I keep coming back to a sunlit two bedroom
I long to but don't want to be Isolde
and I desperately don't want to be Tristan
and I don't want to be the vibration of strings
like the dust of the Little Mermaid

just a girl with a glass of milk
in June in the foothills

In The Meantime

humans war and pillage and murder
but the clouds turn golden each evening
regardless

we create art to keep breathing
lend as many hands as we have
give as much soul as remains
accept life is constant open-heart surgery

stare at the sun in astonishment
remain a little 2 by 2 m² sphere of existence
do our best to save, to have and to hold
our *lovers of the light*

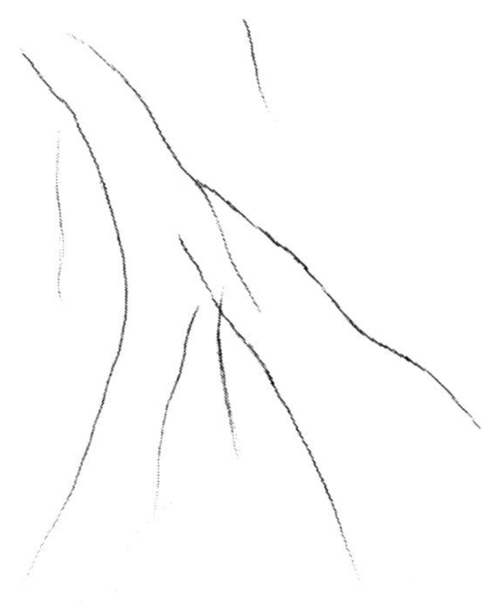

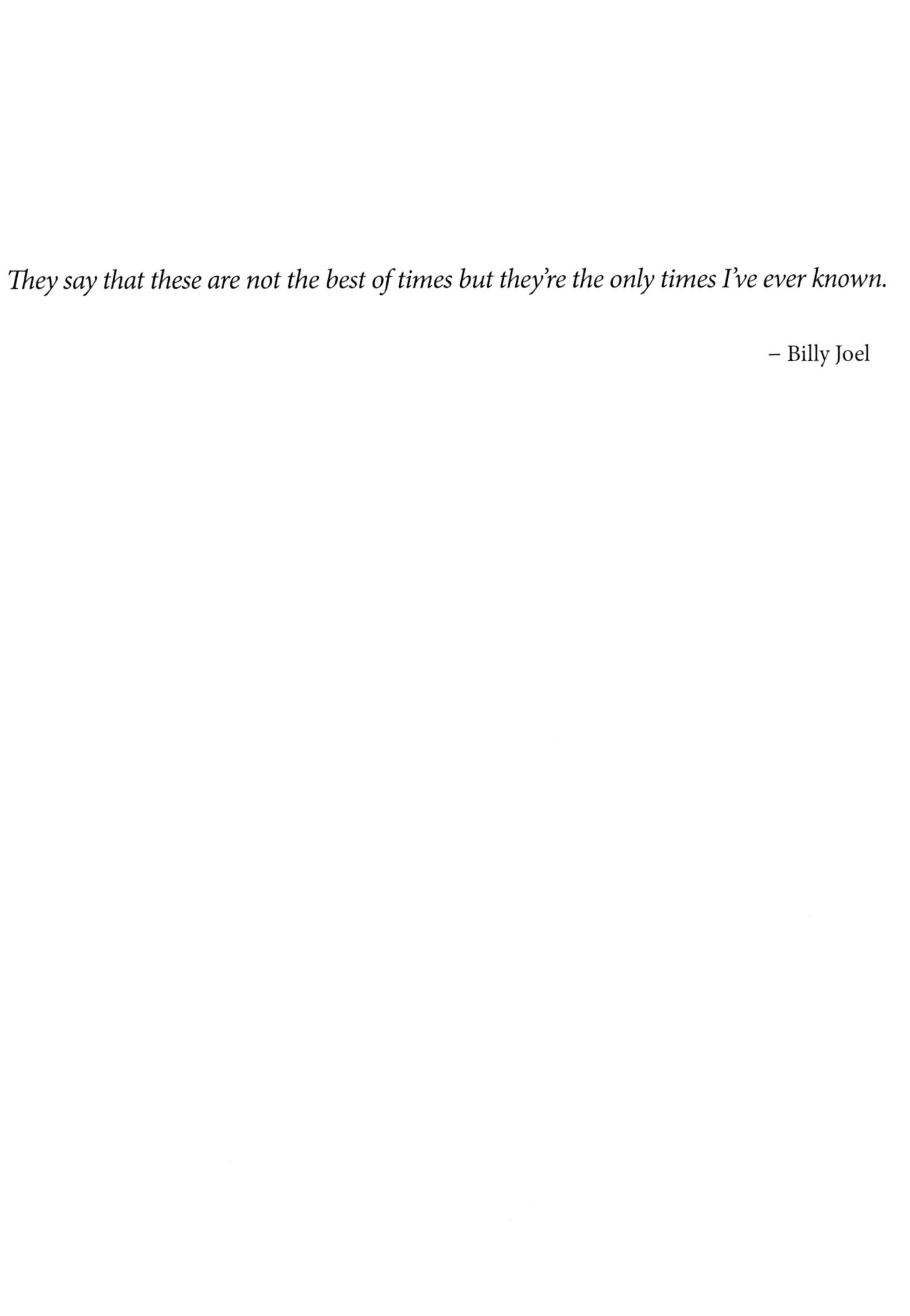

They say that these are not the best of times but they're the only times I've ever known.

– Billy Joel

The italicized titles of poems are citations from the songs:

P. 11 – *Trees Get Wheeled Away* by Bright Eyes
P. 31 – *Babel* by Mumford and Sons
P. 85 – *Hamilton* by Lin Manuel Miranda
P. 95 – *Sweet Nothings* by Taylor Swift
P. 101 – *That Funny Feeling* (from "Inside") by Bo Burnham, also covered by Phoebe Bridgers

This edition is a result of a collaboration with Издателство Фо, Sofia, Bulgaria.

Bibliografische Information der Deutschen Nationalbibliothek
Die Deutsche Nationalbibliothek verzeichnet diese Publikation in der
Deutschen Nationalbibliografie; detaillierte bibliografische Daten sind
im Internet über http://www.dnb.de abrufbar.

ISBN: 978-3-962580-152-7

Umschlag: Sophia Alexandra
Zeichnungen: Sophia Alexandra
Satz: Nicely Media
Druck: Schaltungsdienst Lange, Berlin
Hergestellt in Deutschland

Ganz im Sinne der Nachhaltigkeit wurde diese Publikation
auf FSC-zertifiziertem Papier klimaneutral gedruckt.

PalmArtPress
Verlegerin: Catharine J. Nicely
Pfalzburger Str. 69, 10719 Berlin
www.palmartpress.com

Aus dem Programm von PalmArtPress

Wolfgang Kubin
102 Sonette
ISBN: 978-3-96258-104-6
Gedichte, 128 Seiten, Hardcover, Deutsch

Jutta Habedanck
Mensch Sein, Mansch Sein, mit Gedankenströmen
ISBN: 978-3-96258-045-2
Kunst/Lyrik, 150 Seiten, Klappenbroschur, Deutsch

Juan Ramón Jiménez
Tagebuch eines frischvermählten Dichters
ISBN: 978-3-941524-97-2
Lyrik, 274 Seiten, Hardcover, Übers. Leopold Federmair

Hajo Jahn
Die Facetten des Prinzen Jussuf – Ein Lesebuch über Else Lasker-Schüler
ISBN: 978-3-96258-106-0
Lesebuch, 192 Seiten, mit farb. Abb., Hardcover, Deutsch

Nicanor Parra
Parra Poesie
ISBN: 978-3-941524-78-1
Lyrik Übertragung I. Brökel, mit Abb. Ulrike Ertel, 60 Seiten
Hardcover, Spanisch/Deutsch

Denise Buser
Sechs Beine stolpern nicht
ISBN: 978-3-96258-110-7
Fakten und Fabeln, 200 Seiten, Hardcover, Deutsch

Leopold Federmair
Der unsichtbare Thron
ISBN: 978-3-96258-105-3
Erzählungen, 300 Seiten, Hardcover, Deutsch

Michel Deguy
Wär nicht das Herz
ISBN: 978-3-96258-091-9
Gedichte, Übers. L. Federmair, Nachwort Jean-Luc Nancy, 100 Seiten
Hardcover, Deutsch

Bianca Döring
Schalen
ISBN: 978-3-96258-093-3
Gedichte, 90 Seiten, Hardcover, Deutsch

Sophia Alexandra has been at home in stories and colors for as long as she can remember. She grew up between Germany, Bulgaria and both US coasts. After earning a degree in psychology, she went into designing for film and has worked on independent projects as well as large scale productions in different positions. Poetry has always been her emotional language and English the one where she feels most at ease.